T0069215

# STONE LYRE

"René Char, intrepid explorer of the marvelous, witness to the catastrophe of history, plowman of 'the metered field,' stands revealed in Nancy Naomi Carlson's splendid translations as a guiding spirit of our time, the one who found in the earth 'its secret blood, its calamitous stone.' And the names that he gave to his discoveries sing out in *Stone Lyre*, a book of encounters for the ages."

> —*Christopher Merrill, poet, journalist, and director of the University of Iowa's International Writing Program*

"Great poets deserve many translators, and Nancy Naomi Carlson brings her ear to Char's work in English in a compelling way. Anyone who opens this book... will love her musical use of our language.... (T)his new translation of Char's work... shows us ... the intensity, the dream-like language, the gravity of tone, and the constant impression that one is reading not words in the language, but sparks of flames that defy any attempt at interpretation, or rather open themselves to multiple interpretations at once, clashing with each other, their intersection catching fire."

> —*from the Foreword to* Stone Lyre, *by Ilya Kaminsky, poet and author of* Dancing in Odessa

"Like so many for whom translations are a necessity, I will read Carlson's versions of Char as poems in my own language, including such lines as: 'This at the start of endearing years / I recall the earth loved us a little.' This collection is full of such intense, moving movements, and yet it also has the integrity of a single, singular book. It can teach us a new English."

> —*Bin Ramke, poet and editor of* Denver Quarterly

# STONE LYRE

## POEMS OF RENÉ CHAR

*Selected and translated by Nancy Naomi Carlson*

*With a Foreword by Ilya Kaminsky*

Tupelo Press
North Adams, Massachusetts

**Stone Lyre: Poems of René Char**

The poems in this volume originally appeared in the following books and are used with permission, as noted.

Copyright Éditions Gallimard, Paris:
*Les Matinaux* (1950): "Pyrénées," "Le Carreau," "Les Nuits justes," "L'Amoureuse en secret," "L'Adolescent souffleté," "Anoukis et plus tard Jeanne," "Recours au ruisseau," "Les Lichens," "Toute vie." *Fureur et mystère* (1962): "Congé au vent," "Le Loriot," "Évadné," "Le Martinet," "La Sorgue," "Madeleine à la veilleuse," "Allégeance," "Seuil," "La Campagne du vannier," "Fréquence," "Marthe." *La Parole en archipel* (1962): "Quatre fascinants," "Vers l'arbre-frère aux jours comptés," "La Passe de Lyon," "Marmonnement," "Victoire éclaire," "Invitation," "Pourquoi la journée vole," "La Fauvette des roseaux," "Déclarer son nom," "Éros suspendu," "Fontis." *Le Nu perdu* (1971): "Devancier," "Yvonne," "Lied du figuier," "Lutteurs," "Jeu muet," "Permanent invisible," "Ni éternal ni temporal." *Recherche de la base et du sommet* (1971): "Madeleine qui veillait." *Aromates chasseurs* (1975): "L'Ébriété." *Fenêtres dormantes et porte sur le toit* (1979): "Éprise." *Dehors la nuit est gouvernée* (1983): "Courbet: Les Casseurs de cailloux." *Loin de nos cendres* (1983): "Pour qu'une forêt."

Copyright Librairie Jose Corti, Paris:
*Le Marteau sans Maître* (1934): "Voici," "L'Instituteur révoqué," "Tu ouvres les yeux," "Chaîne," and "Vivante demain."

*Library of Congress Cataloging-in-Publication Data*
Char, René, 1907–1988.
[Poems. English & French. Selections]
Stone lyre : poems of René Char / selected and translated by Nancy Naomi Carlson ; with a foreword by Ilya Kaminsky. – 1st pbk. ed.
     p. cm.
English and French.
ISBN-13: 978-1-932195-78-1 (pbk. : alk. paper)
ISBN-10: 1-932195-78-5 (pbk. : alk. paper)
1. Char, René, 1907-1988--Translations into English. I. Carlson, Nancy Naomi, 1949- II. Title.
PQ2605.H3345A23 2010
841'.912–DC22
2009043979

Cover and text designed by Josef Beery, and composed in Émigré Mrs. Eaves.
Cover photograph: iStockphoto.

Printed in the United States by Lightning Source.
First paperback edition: February 2010.

Tupelo Press
P.O. Box 1767, North Adams, Massachusetts 01247
Telephone: (413) 664–9611 / Fax: (413) 664–9711
editor@tupelopress.org / www.tupelopress.org

Tupelo Press is an award-winning independent literary press that publishes fine fiction, non-fiction, and poetry in books that are a joy to hold as well as read. Tupelo Press is a registered 501(c)3 non-profit organization, and we rely on public support to carry out our mission of publishing extraordinary work that may be outside the realm of the large commercial publishers. Financial donations are welcome and are tax deductible.

Supported in part by an award from the
National Endowment for the Arts

NATIONAL
ENDOWMENT
FOR THE ARTS

For my mother, who has
instilled in me a love for
*tout ce qui est français.*

N.N.C.

# CONTENTS

FOREWORD: ON RENÉ CHAR, BY ILYA KAMINSKY     XI

INTRODUCTION: BY NANCY NAOMI CARLSON     XV

ᵗᵚᵗ     ᵗᵚᵗ     ᵗᵚᵗ

*INVITATION*     INVITATION     3

*CONGÉ AU VENT*     WIND ON FURLOUGH     5

*VICTOIRE ÉCLAIRE*     LIGHTNING VICTORY     7

*LIED DU FIGUIER*     LIED OF THE FIG TREE     9

*LE LORIOT*     THE ORIOLE     11

*QUATRE FASCINANTS*     FOUR WHO CHARM     13

*ÉVADNÉ*     ÉVADNÉ     15

*ALLÉGEANCE*     ALLEGIANCE     17

*MARTHE*     MARTHE     19

*SEUIL*     THRESHOLD     21

*POURQUOI LA JOURNÉE VOLE*     WHY THE DAY STEALS BY     23

*MARMONNEMENT*     MUMBLING     25

*PERMANENT INVISIBLE*     ENDURING INVISIBLE     27

*NI ÉTERNEL NI TEMPOREL*     NOT ETERNAL NOR TEMPORAL     29

*L'ÉBRIÉTÉ*     INEBRIATION     31

*LE MARTINET*     THE SWIFT     33

*MADELEINE À LA VEILLEUSE*    MAGDALENE WITH SMOKING FLAME    35

*MADELEINE QUI VEILLAIT*    MAGDALENE KEEPING WATCH    37

*ÉROS SUSPENDU*    EROS SUSPENDED    41

*LUTTEURS*    COMBATANTS    43

*FRÉQUENCE*    FREQUENCY    45

*RECOURS AU RUISSEAU*    RECOURSE TO OUR STREAM    47

*ANOUKIS ET PLUS TARD JEANNE*    ANOUKIS AND LATER JEANNE    49

*YVONNE*    YVONNE    51

*LA SORGUE*    THE SORGUE    53

*DÉCLARER SON NOM*    PROCLAIMING ONE'S NAME    55

*L'ADOLESCENT SOUFFLETÉ*    THE SLAPPED ADOLESCENT    57

*JEU MUET*    MUTE GAME    59

*VOICI*    HERE    61

*TU OUVRES LES YEUX*    YOU OPEN YOUR EYES    63

*FONTIS*    FONTIS    65

*LES NUITS JUSTES*    RIGHTEOUS NIGHTS    67

*LE CARREAU*    THE WINDOWPANE    69

*PYRÉNÉES*    PYRENEES    71

*VIVANTE DEMAIN*    ALIVE TOMORROW    73

*POUR QU'UNE FORÊT...*    NO FOREST...    75

*CHAÎNE*    CHAIN    77

*L'INSTITUTEUR RÉVOQUÉ*    THE DISMISSED INSTRUCTOR    79

*TOUTE VIE*    EVERY LIFE    81

*VERS L'ARBRE-FRÈRE AUX JOURS COMPTÉS*
     TO BROTHER-TREE OF NUMBERED DAYS    83

*ÉPRISE*    IN LOVE    85

*LA PASSE DE LYON*    REACHING LYON    87

*LA COMPAGNE DU VANNIER*    THE BASKET WEAVER'S WIFE    89

*LA FAUVETTE DES ROSEAUX*    SONGBIRD AMONG THE REEDS    91

*L'AMOUREUSE EN SECRET*    SECRET LOVE    93

*LES LICHENS*    LICHENS    95

*DEVANCIER*    ANCESTOR    97

*COURBET: LES CASSEURS DE CAILLOUX*
     COURBET: THE STONE BREAKERS    99

ᕤ    ᕤ    ᕤ

ACKNOWLEDGMENTS    100

# FOREWORD
*by Ilya Kaminsky*

## On René Char

> *This at the start of endearing years*
> *I recall the earth loved us a little*

DURING WORLD WAR TWO, the poet René Char found himself, under the *nom de guerre* Captain Alexandre, in charge of the underground Resistance to the Nazis in the Bases-Alpes region of southern France. He kept a journal that he called "Leaves of Hypnos," named after the Greek divinity for sleep, son of night and brother of death. These conditions of sleep, death, and divine origin reappear often in *Stone Lyre*, this new collection of poems by a poet who once said he aimed for "transhumance of the Word."

꙾ ꙾ ꙾

First, a few biographical details: The poet, whose surname was an abbreviated form of Charlemagne, was born on June 14, 1907, the only son of a manufacturer who also served as mayor of Isle-sur-Sorgue. When René Emile Char was eleven years old, his father died. By the time he reached his sixteenth year, Char had written his earliest known poem, "Jouvence," and in his twenty-first year he published his debut book, *Les Clouches surlecoeur*. One year later, in 1929, he completed his second volume, *Arsenal*, which was praised by the Surrealists, whose ranks he joined by signing *Le Manifeste du Surréalisme*. Char valued the Surrealists' notion of poetry as spontaneous activity and their vision of restlessness as a necessity for a poet; his close association with the movement continued for five years, until 1934, when he renounced the Surrealists, raging against what he saw as their failure to fuse imagination and reality, and following his own conviction that poetry must be free of limits imposed by any ideology or affiliation.

In his wartime writings, as a leader in the Resistance movement, he attempted to describe the inner lives of those under his command.

Although before the war Char was little known in France, his publication of *Seuls demeurent* in 1945 resulted in wide acclaim. His work in the following years involved stylistic innovation, as he omitted from his poetry most personal references, aiming to present with lyric intensity the inner experience of "everyman." As his work began to receive critical recognition internationally, Char continued to refuse any discussion of personal experiences, hoping that interpretations of his poetry would not be limited to details of his historical existence. His focus, instead, was on the poet's moral responsibility, an emphasis reflected in his activities in the Resistance and, in later years, in his work against nuclear proliferation.

※    ※    ※

We must take Char's cue and abandon biographical details here in favor of considering his poetics. Poets' biographies, after all, consist of their reading lists. Char adored Reverdy in his youth, and throughout his life he often admitted admiration for Baudelaire, Rimbaud, Mallarmé, Apollinaire, and Valéry. A closer look at his work also shows the influence of German poets such as Hölderlin, Rilke, and perhaps Trakl. Outside of the circle of poets, there is a clear influence of Nietzsche's writings, and of the ancient Greek philosopher Heraclitus, whom Char seems to have regarded as a poet and mythologist as much as a critical thinker.

Char's work, too, attempts to create mythology, particularly in his writings about animals, but even more than mythology, one feels that Char is trying to make up an autonomous language—poetry that is, "at once, speech and silent." He is trying to reach a moment when one could perhaps say, "and the earth, through me, ceased to die."

"The best work," Valéry wrote, "is that which keeps its secret longest." And Char's writing is filled with secret language. At times it is surreal, dark ("I dig in the air my grave"), piercing us in a way Paul Celan's lines do; at other moments, Char's lines attempt to embrace the earth around them ("my love infuses the streets of the town"); but always in his work there is a continual charge of privacy, of intimacy: dream-speech, song of a whisperer, a clunk of a bone on bone. "The truth," he tells us, "is in the blade."

Reading these poems, one is particularly drawn to Char's bestiary of charms for the animals, in which the poet summons chant to replenish intensity in narrative, to catch the lyric impulse at the source of animal myths. Char's animals live in constant danger—yet the hunter adds to the beauty of the prey. Stevens's "death is the mother of beauty" comes to mind often, as these lyrics of bulls, trout, snakes, and larks attest "it is never night when you die."

↜  ↜  ↜

Char has been lucky with English translators, as such talented authors as William Carlos Williams, Samuel Beckett, James Wright, Cid Corman, and Paul Auster, among many others, have translated his work. What can a new translation add to this company? Great poets, admittedly, deserve many translators, and Nancy Naomi Carlson brings her ear to Char's work in English in a compelling way. Anyone who opens this book on "To Brother-Tree of Numbered Days" will love her musical use of our language:

> *Larch tree's brief harp*
> *On the spur of moss and flagstones in seed*

*—Forest's facade where clouds break apart—*
*Counterpoint paired to the void in which I believe.*

One more biographical detail, before you embark on a journey of passion and gravitas. As his dedicated and attentive scholar Mary Ann Caws relates, Char described the psychological atmosphere of his childhood, presenting an unforgettable picture of his parents: "My father had courteous, shining eyes, good and never possessive…. My mother seemed to touch everything and to reach nothing, at once busy, indolent, and sure of herself. The strong lines of their contrasting natures clashed with each other, their intersection catching fire."

What I find most interesting about this new translation of Char's work in English is how it shows us the poet's stylistic unity over the years—the intensity, the dream-like language, the gravity of tone, and the constant impression that one is reading not words in a language but sparks of flames that defy any attempt at interpretation, or rather that open themselves to multiple interpretations at once, clashing with each other, their intersection catching fire.

# INTRODUCTION

*by Nancy Naomi Carlson, Translator*

YEARS AGO, I purchased a Dell classic entitled *French Poetry from Baudelaire to the Present*. The "present" was 1971, and René Char, along with Yves Bonnefoy, was one of the "younger" poets included in this slight volume.

At the time, I was unable to grasp the meaning of the aphorism included in that volume's four-piece sampling of Char's work: "If potatoes no longer grow in the ground, on this ground we will dance. It is our right and our frivolity."

Even today, reading these words on their brittle and yellowed page, I am not convinced I completely understand them, but over the years I have gained a deep appreciation for the mystery that pervades Char's aphorisms, his dense prose poems, and his poems utilizing line breaks. Moreover, I continue to be fascinated by Char himself—a remarkable and charismatic man who dared to marry a Jew in 1932 despite the growing wave of anti-Semitism; who signed Breton's anti-Fascist manifesto; who risked his life fighting in the French Resistance movement; who protested against nuclear proliferation into his old age; and who enjoyed the respect and friendship of such literary giants as Albert Camus, Octavio Paz, and William Carlos Williams.

The poems included in this translation give a representative sampling of Char's oeuvre, chosen from collections whose publication dates span a range of close to fifty years. I was particularly drawn to the unusual imagery of his love poems, such as "Évadné," "Marthe," "Lichens," "Reaching Lyon," "The Basket Weaver's Wife," and "Secret Love." Poems that feature birds (orioles, songbirds, swifts, larks) also appealed to me because of their lyric intensity.

Despite the variety of themes in these poems, they all presented a similar challenge: How to find ways of creating translations that remain faithful to Char's original meaning—at times relatively inaccessible—without easing the reader's path by making semantic leaps. For example, I found the following two lines written by Char to be among the most mysterious and puzzling of all, but made no attempt to make them more understandable: "A thousand years weigh less than a corpse on my lyre" ("Invitation") and "Lepers descend with the slow snow" ("Lightning Victory").

Another challenge was to make sense of Char's ambiguous use of the third person possessive. In French, both "son" and "sa" refer to either "his" or "her," depending on what noun is being modified. For example, "son livre" can be translated as either "his book" or "her book," depending on the context. Char's poem "Yvonne," written in memory of Yvonne Zervos, one of Char's intimate friends, illustrates this ambiguity. Here is the poem in its entirety in both languages.

### *YVONNE*
La Soif hospitalière

*Qui l'entendit jamais se plaindre ?*

*Nulle autre qu'elle n'aurait pu boire sans mourir les*
    *quarante fatigues,*
*Attendre, loin devant, ceux qui viendront après;*
*De l'éveil au couchant sa manoeuvre était mâle.*

*Qui a creusé le puits et hisse l'eau gisante*
*Risque son coeur dans l'écart de ses mains.*

*YVONNE*
Welcoming thirst

*Who heard her ever complain?*

*Only she could drink and survive forty rounds,*
*Could wait, worlds beyond, for those coming next;*
*From waking to sunset, used tactics of men.*

*Whoever dug the shaft and raises water from rest*
*Risks her heart in the well of her hands.*

The poem describes the "male" qualities of Yvonne, including how much alcohol she could consume, and how she used the "tactics of men." Then comes the last stanza with its ambiguities of "son coeur" and "ses mains." Whose heart is it? Whose hands? Do they refer to the person digging the shaft and holding the water? Is this person a man or a woman? Do they refer to Yvonne? Do they refer to the same person? I chose to use "her" in both instances to maintain the sense of mystery. To have used "her heart" and "his hands" or any other combination seemed somehow too simplistic.

Char is fond of leaving out punctuation, which also contributes to the sense of mystery. I chose to omit punctuation in the poems where Char did so, such as "Évadné," "Alive Tomorrow," "Chain," and "Courbet: The Stone Breakers." By leaving out punctuation, I was not tempted to clear up any syntactical confusion where I might have inadvertently imposed my own meaning on Char's lines. For example, in "Chaîne," it is not clear if the line "Sur la paille des fatalistes" ("On the straw of those who believe in fate") refers to the line that precedes it or follows it, and I maintained this ambiguity:

*Les labours rayonnants adorent les guérisseurs détrempés*
*Sur la paille des fatalistes*
*L'écume d'astre coule tout allumée*

*Tilled fields radiate, worship sweat-drenched healers*
*On the straw of those who believe in fate*
*Flows the foam of ignited stars*

An added difficulty in translating Char's work was my conscious effort to maintain the music of his line—to keep the text "beautiful." French is inherently musical by virtue of its rhythm and repetition of sound. Most French words stress the last syllable. To preserve the rhythm of the French, I tried to end each line with English words that stressed the last syllable or were mono-syllabic. For example, in "Vers l'arbre-frère aux jours comptés," all words found at the end of each line stress the last syllable:

## VERS L'ARBRE-FRÈRE
## AUX JOURS COMPTÉS

*Harpe brève des mélèzes,*
*Sur l'éperon de mousse et de dalles en germe*
*—Façade des forêts où casse le nuage—*
*Contrepoint du vide auquel je crois.*

I replicated this pattern in my translation:

## TO BROTHER-TREE
## OF NUMBERED DAYS

*Larch tree's brief harp*
*On the spur of moss and flagstones in seed*
*—Forest's façade where clouds break apart—*
*Counterpoint paired to the void in which I believe.*

In the case of Char's prose poems, I also attempted to end each sentence with a stressed syllable, in keeping with the original French.

## CONGÉ AU VENT

À flancs de coteau du village bivouaquent des champs fournis de mimosas. À l'époque de la cueillette, il arrive que, loin de leur endroit, on fasse la rencontre extrêmement odorante d'une fille dont les bras se sont occupés durant la journée aux fragiles branches. Pareille à une lampe dont l'auréole de clarté serait de parfum, elle s'en va, le dos tourné au soleil couchant.

Il serait sacrilège de lui adresser la parole.

L'espadrille foulant l'herbe, cédez-lui le pas du chemin. Peut-être aurez-vous la chance de distinguer sur ses lèvres la chimère de l'humidité de la Nuit?

## WIND ON FURLOUGH

Flanking the hills of the village, fields thick with mimosa pitch camp. On harvest days, miles away, you may find yourself stunned by the sweetest of scents—a girl whose arms have held those delicate blooms since dawn. Like a lamp that radiates perfumed light, she goes her way, out of the setting sun.

Sacrilege to utter a single word.

Yield her the path as you hear her espadrilles crush the grass. With luck you'll detect on her lips the humid kiss of night.

In addition to ending lines and sentences with stressed syllables to preserve the original French rhythm, I made every attempt to use no more than two unstressed syllables in a row, as is characteristic of the Char poems. This constraint was, perhaps, the hardest. I found myself facing the dilemma of having to choose between meaning and music again and again. In some cases I reversed lines, or reversed words in a line in order to maintain both the meaning and the music. Often I changed the syntax. For example, here are the opening stanzas of "Invitation" in both French and English where the syntax has been changed from the original French, but the music remains:

> *J'appelle les amours qui roués et suivis par la faulx de l'été,*
> *au soir embaument l'air de leur blanche inaction.*

> *I summon the loves—pursued and tortured by summer's scythe—*
> *whose white torpor embalms the night air.*

French is known for its rich repetition of sound, even in everyday speech. Throughout my translations, I tried to replicate this texture through generous internal and end-of-line slant rhyme and perfect rhyme, often duplicating the French sounds in the English version. However, one particular French vowel, often appearing as "é," posed a great challenge for me, since it does not exist in English but occurs in many French words, independent of their spelling or part of speech—e.g., étranger (stranger) / années (years) / parler (to speak) / séparé (separated) / pieds (feet). I was able to approximate this sound with words containing "ay" such as "play" or "raise." For "Pyrénées," a poem of 12 lines, 7 of which end with this sound as the stressed syllable, I ended each line with an English word containing an approximation of this sound:

### PYRÉNÉES

> *Montagne des grands abusés,*
> *Au sommet de vos tours fiévreuses*
> *Faiblit la dernière clarté.*

> *Rien que le vide et l'avalanche,*
> *La détresse et le regret!*

*Tous ces troubadours mal-aimés*
*Ont vu blanchir dans un été*
*Leur doux royaume pessimiste.*

*Ah! la neige est inexorable*
*Qui aime qu'on souffre à ses pieds,*
*Qui veut que l'on meure glacé*
*Quand on a vécu dans les sables.*

## PYRENEES

*Mountain chain of misled greats,*
*Atop your fevered peaks*
*The last light fails.*

*Only anguish and avalanche,*
*Rift and regret.*

*These minstrels full of ache*
*Have seen their meek kingdom fade—*
*Hopeless and blanched in one summer.*

*Ah! The snow never forgives—*
*Loves us to writhe in pain,*
*Wants us to die, bodies glazed,*
*When we have survived desert sands.*

I especially enjoyed translating poems that employed perfect end-rhyme couplets. For example, "La Sorgue" contains the following couplets: "compagnon / passion;" "maison / raison;" "équarrisseurs / menteur;" "éclos / chapeau." I used slant rhyme as follows: "friend / land;" "begins / brink;" "fools / lies;" "hat / hatched." In some cases, I tried to reproduce the alliteration found in the lines, reproducing the exact sound found in the French, wherever possible. For example, "The Windowpane" starts with "pures pluies." I translated these words as "pure downpours," maintaining the "p" of the

French, although placing the second "p" in the middle of the second word, rather than as the initial consonant.

Choosing a title for this collection was daunting. I knew I wanted something that would convey the dynamic quality of a balancing of opposites, as is often the case within and among individual poems by Char, including lucidity and fantasy, as well as the horror and beauty of life. *Stone Lyre* seemed particularly fitting. In several poems "rock / death / hardship" contrasts with "music / life / freedom" ("Courbet: The Stone Breakers," "Songbird Among the Reeds"). Throughout this collection many poems refer to stone, including stonecutters ("Invitation," "Ancestor"), flagstones ("To Brother-Tree of Numbered Days"), stones sealed in walls ("In Love"), and rocks ("Lichens," "Anoukis and Later Jeanne"). Two poems refer to lyres ("Invitation," "Évadné"). Many other poems refer to music, such as the hum of algae ("Frequency"), a chanting sun ("Proclaiming One's Name"), a trumpet ("Eros"), skylarks ("Four Who Charm," "Not Eternal Nor Temporal,"), orioles ("The Oriole"),  and "food like an oboe's reed" ("Secret Love").

Elaine Marks, the editor of my old Dell paperback, concludes that Char's potato aphorism presents an image that "is not a retrospective experience but a starting point...so that the poem continues in the reader's mind as a lived and personal experience."

For me, Char's words are as relevant today as when written. They keep inviting me back to dance—my right and my frivolity.

# STONE LYRE

## *INVITATION*

*J'appelle les amours qui roués et suivis par la faulx de l'été, au soir embaument l'air de leur blanche inaction.*

*Il n'y a plus de cauchemar, douce insomnie perpétuelle. Il n'y a plus d'aversion. Que la pause d'un bal dont l'entrée est partout dans les nuées du ciel.*

*Je viens avant la rumeur des fontaines, au final du tailleur de pierre.*

*Sur ma lyre mille ans pèsent moins qu'un mort.*

*J'appelle les amants.*

## INVITATION

I summon the loves—pursued and tortured by summer's scythe—whose white torpor embalms the night air.

No more nightmare—sleeplessness, endless and sweet. No more spite. Only the pause in a dance whose entrance pervades the fleece of clouds in the sky.

I come before the rush of springs, when the stonecutter's work is done.

A thousand years weigh less than a corpse on my lyre.

I summon the lovers.

## CONGÉ AU VENT

À flancs de coteau du village bivouaquent des champs fournis de mimosas. À l'époque de la cueillette, il arrive que, loin de leur endroit, on fasse la rencontre extrêmement odorante d'une fille dont les bras se sont occupés durant la journée aux fragiles branches. Pareille à une lampe dont l'auréole de clarté serait de parfum, elle s'en va, le dos tourné au soleil couchant.

Il serait sacrilège de lui adresser la parole.

L'espadrille foulant l'herbe, cédez-lui le pas du chemin. Peut-être aurez-vous la chance de distinguer sur ses lèvres la chimère de l'humidité de la Nuit?

## WIND ON FURLOUGH

Flanking the hills of the village, fields thick with mimosa pitch camp. On harvest days, miles away, you may find yourself stunned by the sweetest of scents—a girl whose arms have held those delicate blooms since dawn. Like a lamp that radiates perfumed light, she goes her way, out of the setting sun.

Sacrilege to utter a single word.

Yield her the path as you hear her espadrilles crush the grass. With luck you'll detect on her lips the humid kiss of night.

## VICTOIRE ÉCLAIR

*L'oiseau bêche la terre,*
*Le serpent sème,*
*La mort améliorée*
*Applaudit la récolte.*

*Pluton dans le ciel!*

*L'explosion en nous.*
*Là seulement dans moi.*
*Fol et sourd, comment pourrais-je l'être davantage?*

*Plus de second soi-même, de visage changeant, plus de saison pour la flamme*
*et de saison pour l'ombre!*

*Avec la lente neige descendent les lépreux.*
*Soudain l'amour, l'égal de la terreur,*
*D'une main jamais vue arrête l'incendie, redresse le soleil, reconstruit*
*l'Amie.*

*Rien n'annonçait une existence si forte.*

## LIGHTNING VICTORY

The bird spades the earth,
The serpent sows,
Death, seasoned,
Hails the harvest.

Pluto rules the sky!

Inside us, explosion.
Inside me alone.
Insane and deaf, how could I be more so?

Gone, second self, fickle face, season of flame
    and season of shade!

Lepers descend with the slow snow.

In a flash, love—equal of dread—
With an unseen hand, contains the blaze, restores
    the sun, recasts the beloved.

Nothing augured a being so bold.

*LIED DU FIGUIER*

*Tant il gela que les branches laiteuses*
*Molestèrent la scie, se cassèrent aux mains.*
*Le printemps ne vit pas verdir les gracieuses.*

*Le figuier demanda au maître du gisant*
*L'arbuste d'une foi nouvelle.*
*Mais le loriot, son prophète,*
*L'aube chaude de son retour,*
*En se posant sur le désastre,*
*Au lieu de faim, périt d'amour.*

## LIED OF THE FIG TREE

So deep a freeze that milky branches
Damaged the saw and snapped in the hands.
Spring did not see the gracious ones turn green.

From the keeper of those who fall,
The fig tree asked for a new faith's shrub.
But its prophet, the oriole—
Warm dawn of his flight home—
Alighting on this unfortunate ruin,
Instead of hunger, died of love.

## *LE LORIOT*

*Le loriot entra dans la capitale de l'aube.*
*L'épée de son chant ferma le lit triste.*
*Tout à jamais prit fin.*

## THE ORIOLE

The oriole breached dawn's capital town.
The sword of his song closed the cheerless bed.
All forever came to an end.

## QUATRE FASCINANTS

### I. Le Taureau

Il ne fait jamais nuit quand tu meurs,
Cerné de ténèbres qui crient,
Soleil aux deux pointes semblables.

Fauve d'amour, vérité dans l'épée,
Couple qui se poignarde unique parmi tous.

### II. La Truite

Rives qui croulez en parure
Afin d'emplir tout le miroir,
Gravier où balbutie la barque
Que le courant presse et retrousse,
Herbe, herbe toujours étirée,
Herbe, herbe jamais en répit,
Que devient votre créature
Dans les orages transparents
Où son coeur la précipita?

### III. Le Serpent

Prince des contresens, exerce mon amour
À tourner son Seigneur que je hais de n'avoir
Que trouble répression ou fastueux espoir.

Revanche à tes couleurs, débonnaire serpent,
Sous le couvert du bois, et en toute maison.
Par le lien qui unit la lumière à la peur,
Tu fais semblant de fuir, ô serpent marginal!

### IV. L'Alouette

Extrême braise du ciel et première ardeur du jour,
Elle reste sertie dans l'aurore et chante la terre agitée,
Carillon maître de son haleine et libre de sa route.

Fascinante, on la tue en l'émerveillant.

# FOUR WHO CHARM

### I. The Bull

It is never dark when you die,
Encircled by shrieking shades,
Twin-pierced sun.

Love's brutal beast, truth in the blade,
Singular pair, by each other impaled.

### II. The Trout

Riverbanks, you who collapse
Adorned to fill the mirror;
Gravel below the babbling boat
Embraced and released by the stream;
Grass, grass always endlessly stretched,
Grass, grass never left to rest,
What is in store for your creature
Whose heart has propelled her
Amid the transparent storms?

### III. The Snake

Prince of distortion, induce my love
To foil her Lord, the one
I hate—his somber suppression, gaudy hope.

May your colors prevail, stately snake,
Under cover of wood and in every home.
By the line joining fear and light,
O snake made for margins, you feign flight.

### IV. The Lark

Sky's last ember and day's first fire,
Gem set in dawn, she sings of the restless earth,
Carillon master of breath and free to fly.

She who charms is charmed to death.

RENÉ CHAR

## *ÉVADNÉ*

*L'été et notre vie étions d'un seul tenant*
*La campagne mangeait la couleur de ta jupe odorante*
*Avidité et contrainte s'étaient réconciliées*
*Le château de Maubec s'enfonçait dans l'argile*
*Bientôt s'effondrerait le roulis de sa lyre*
*La violence des plantes nous faisait vaciller*
*Un corbeau rameur sombre déviant de l'escadre*
*Sur le muet silex de midi écartelé*
*Accompagnait notre entente aux mouvements tendres*
*La faucille partout devait se reposer*
*Notre rareté commençait un règne*
*(Le vent insomnieux qui nous ride la paupière*
*En tournant chaque nuit la page consentie*
*Veut que chaque part de toi que je retienne*
*Soit étendue à un pays d'âge affamé et de larmier géant)*

*C'était au début d'adorables années*
*La terre nous aimait un peu je me souviens.*

# ÉVADNÉ

Summer and our life, we were fused
Fields devoured the hues of your perfumed clothes
Restraint and passion declared a truce
Maubec Castle was sinking in loam
Soon the ring of its lyre would cease
The violence of plants made us reel
A crow—gloomy rower—veering from the fleet
On the quartered noon of silent flint
Beat time with tender wings for our détente
Nowhere were signs of the sickle
Our rarity ushered in a new reign
(Insomniac wind that ripples the lids of our eyes
While turning each night the consenting page
Desires each part of you I retain
Be deployed to a land of famished age and towering dripstone)

This at the start of endearing years
I recall the earth loved us a little.

## ALLÉGEANCE

*Dans les rues de la ville il y a mon amour. Peu importe où il va dans le temps divisé. Il n'est plus mon amour, chacun peut lui parler. Il ne se souvient plus; qui au juste l'aima?*

*Il cherche son pareil dans le voeu des regards. L'espace qu'il parcourt est ma fidélité. Il dessine l'espoir et léger l'éconduit. Il est prépondérant sans qu'il y prenne part.*

*Je vis au fond de lui comme une épave heureuse. À son insu, ma solitude est son trésor. Dans le grand méridien où s'inscrit son essor, ma liberté le creuse.*

*Dans les rues de la ville il y a mon amour. Peu importe où il va dans le temps divisé. Il n'est plus mon amour, chacun peut lui parler. Il ne se souvient plus; qui au juste l'aima et l'éclaire de loin pour qu'il ne tombe pas?*

## ALLEGIANCE

My love infuses the streets of the town. Small matter where she moves in divided time. No longer my love, and all are free to pursue her perfume. She no longer remembers—who exactly loved her?

She seeks her match in eyes steeped in desire. She traverses the space of my faithfulness—hope traced, then dismissed. She prevails without taking part.

I live in her depths—blissful sunken wreck—my aloneness her unknown treasure. My freedom burrows deep in the great meridian joined to her flight.

My love infuses the streets of the town. Small matter where she moves in divided time. No longer my love, and all are free to pursue her perfume. She no longer remembers—who exactly loved her and lights her way from afar to prevent a fall?

## MARTHE

Marthe que ces vieux murs ne peuvent pas s'approprier, fontaine où se mire ma monarchie solitaire, comment pourrais-je jamais vous oublier puisque je n'ai pas à me souvenir de vous: vous êtes le présent qui s'accumule. Nous nous unirons sans avoir à nous aborder, à nous prévoir comme deux pavots font en amour une anémone géante.

Je n'entrerai pas dans votre coeur pour limiter sa mémoire. Je ne retiendrai pas votre bouche pour l'empêcher de s'entrouvrir sur le bleu de l'air et la soif de partir. Je veux être pour vous la liberté et le vent de la vie qui passe le seuil de toujours avant que la nuit ne devienne introuvable.

## MARTHE

Never mortar to these walls, Marthe, you are the spring that reflects my lonely reign. How could I ever forget you since you are the present that gathers and grows. Our union will be from afar, unplanned: two pressed poppies that form one great anemone.

I will not enter your heart to limit its memory, nor hold back your lips from their parting on blueness of air and the thirst to leave. For you, let me be freedom and life's wind that carries you over the threshold of *always*—while night can still be found.

## SEUIL

Quand s'ébranla le barrage de l'homme, aspiré par la faille géante de l'abandon du divin, des mots dans le lointain, des mots qui ne voulaient pas se perdre, tentèrent de résister à l'exorbitante poussée. Là se décida la dynastie de leur sens.

J'ai couru jusqu'à l'issue de cette nuit diluvienne. Planté dans le flageolant petit jour, ma ceinture pleine de saisons, je vous attends, ô mes amis qui allez venir. Déjà je vous devine derrière la noirceur de l'horizon. Mon âtre ne tarit pas de voeux pour vos maisons. Et mon bâton de cyprès rit de tout son coeur pour vous.

## THRESHOLD

When the man-made dam gave way, sucked down by that gaping fault—the desertion of gods—words in the distance, words afraid to be lost, tried to resist the ruthless force. It was here their meaning's dynasty took root.

I have run to the end of this long, diluvial night. Planted in quaking dawn, I await you, dear friends who are coming, seasons filling my belt. I divine your presence already, behind the horizon's dark. My hearth never ceases to wish your homes well, and for you, my stroke of cypress laughs with all its heart.

## POURQUOI LA JOURNÉE VOLE

*Le poète s'appuie, durant le temps de sa vie, à quelque arbre, ou mer, ou talus, ou nuage d'une certaine teinte, un moment, si la cironstance le veut. Il n'est pas soudé à l'égarement d'autrui. Son amour, son saisir, son bonheur ont leur équivalent dans tous les lieux où il n'est pas allé, où jamais il n'ira, chez les étrangers qu'il ne connaîtra pas. Lorsqu'on élève la voix devant lui, qu'on le presse d'accepter des égards qui retiennent, si l'on invoque à son propos les astres, il répond qu'il est du pays d'à côté, du ciel qui vient d'être englouti.*

*Le poète vivifie puis court au dénouement.*

*Au soir, malgré sur sa joue plusieurs fossettes d'apprenti, c'est un passant courtois qui brusque les adieux pour être là quand le pain sort du four.*

## WHY THE DAY STEALS BY

The poet leans on some tree, or sea, or slope, or cloud of a certain hue for a moment during his life, if circumstance smoothes the road. He's not welded to others' confusion. His love, his grasp, his joy have their match in all places he's never been, nor will ever go, in strangers he'll never know. When they ply him with prizes—those that would bind—and praise him with voices raised, invoking the stars, he responds that he comes from the country *next door*, from the sky just now engulfed.

The poet gives life then runs to the plot's dénouement.

At night, despite dimples in cheeks like a novice, he cuts short his goodbyes—polite passerby—to be there when the bread leaves the oven.

## MARMONNEMENT

*Pour ne pas me rendre et pour m'y retrouver, je t'offense, mais combien je suis épris de toi, loup, qu'on dit à tort funèbre, pétri des secrets de mon arrière-pays. C'est dans une masse d'amour légendaire que tu laisses la déchaussure vierge, pourchassée, de ton ongle. Loup, je t'appelle, mais tu n'as pas de réalité nommable. De plus, tu es inintelligible. Non-comparant, compensateur, que sais-je? Derrière ta course sans crinière, je saigne, je pleure, je m'enserre de terreur, j'oublie, je ris sous les arbres. Traque impitoyable où l'on s'acharne, où tout est mis en action contre la double proie: toi invisible et moi vivace.*

*Continue, va, nous durons ensemble; et ensemble, bien que séparés, nous bondissons par-dessus le frisson de la suprême déception pour briser la glace des eaux vives et se reconnaître là.*

## MUMBLING

Not to surrender, no, but to find my place I offend you—adored wolf—wrongly described as funereal, molded from secrets breathed in my backwoods. In a mound of fabled love, you leave the mark—virgin and hunted down—of your claw. I call you wolf, but yours is no nameable being, cannot be grasped. With no common scale, no balancing, what do I know? Behind your maneless chase, I bleed, I weep, I writhe in fear, I forget, I laugh under the trees. Ruthless pursuit without end against the double prey: you invisible, me perennial.

Carry on, keep going, together we'll endure; apart, though together, we leap past the shiver of pure deceit, shatter the ice of spring tides, reclaim our reflected selves.

## PERMANENT INVISIBLE

*Permanent invisible aux chasses convoitées,*
*Proche, proche invisible et si proche à mes doigts,*
*Ô mon distant gibier la nuit où je m'abaisse*
*Pour un novice corps à corps.*
*Boire frileusement, être brutal répare.*
*Sur ce double jardin s'arrondit ton couvercle.*
*Tu as la densité de la rose qui se fera.*

## ENDURING INVISIBLE

Enduring invisible—coveted prize of the hunt,
Brushes close, invisible, brushes past my touch,
O my elusive prey, the night where I stoop
For a novice in combat hand to hand.
To shiver and drink, to be savage, restores.
Your cover arches above this twinned garden.
You are as dense as the rose yet to be.

## NI ÉTERNEL NI TEMPOREL

Ô le blé vert dans une terre qui n'a pas encore sué, qui n'a fait que grelotter!
À distance heureuse des soleils précipités des fins de vie. Rasant sous la longue
nuit. Abreuvé d'eau sur sa lumineuse couleur. Pour garde et pour viatique
deux poignards de chevet: l'alouette, l'oiseau qui se pose, le corbeau, l'esprit
qui se grave.

## NOT ETERNAL NOR TEMPORAL

O wheat in May, green in the shivering earth that has never known sweat. A happy distance from diving suns of the ends of lives. Low-lying under the long night. Color glows, watered. For vigil and last rites, two bedside blades: the skylark, bird who alights, and the crow, the spirit engraving itself.

## L'ÉBRIÉTÉ

*Tandis que la moisson achevait de se graver sur le cuivre du soleil, une alouette chantait dans la faille du grand vent sa jeunesse qui allait prendre fin. L'aube d'automne parée de ses miroirs déchirés de coups de feu, dans trois mois retentirait.*

## INEBRIATION

While the harvest engraved itself on the sun's copper face, a skylark's song filled cracks in the great wind. She trilled her youth as it fell away. In three months' time, frosted dawn, mirrors laced with birdshot, would resound.

## LE MARTINET

Martinet aux ailes trop larges, qui vire et crie sa joie autour de la maison. Tel est le coeur.

Il dessèche le tonnerre. Il sème dans le ciel serein. S'il touche au sol, il se déchire.

Sa repartie est l'hirondelle. Il déteste la familière. Que vaut dentelle de la tour?

Sa pause est au creux le plus sombre. Nul n'est plus à l'étroit que lui.

L'été de la longue clarté, il filera dans les ténèbres, par les persiennes de minuit.

Il n'est pas d'yeux pour le tenir. Il crie, c'est toute sa présence. Un mince fusil va l'abattre. Tel est le coeur.

## THE SWIFT

Swift with wings too bold, pumping and shrieking joy as he circles the house. Just like the heart.

Thunder withers before him. He sows in the placid sky. If he touches ground, he will tear apart.

He scorns the swallow, her commonness. What use lace from the tower?

In the darkest of hollows, he finds his narrow respite, where none fits better than he.

In the long brilliance of summer, he streaks his way in shadows, through midnight's shutters.

No eyes can hold him. His presence is only his shriek. A slender gun is going to bring him down. Just like the heart.

## MADELEINE À LA VEILLEUSE
### par Georges de La Tour

*Je voudrais aujourd'hui que l'herbe fût blanche pour fouler l'évidence de vous voir souffrir: je ne regarderais pas sous votre main si jeune la forme dure, sans crépi de la mort. Un jour discrétionnaire, d'autres pourtant moins avides que moi, retireront votre chemise de toile, occuperont votre alcôve. Mais ils oublieront en partant de noyer la veilleuse et un peu d'huile se répandra par le poignard de la flamme sur l'impossible solution.*

## MAGDALENE WITH SMOKING FLAME

*After the painting by Georges de La Tour*

To trample the signs of seeing you suffer, I'd wish today for snow-covered grass: I'd turn away from death's form—crude and harsh—under your tender hand. One capricious day, others, though less avid than I, will remove your canvas blouse, will invade your alcove. But leaving, they will forget to smother the light, and a drop of oil from the dagger of flame will fuel the imagined solution.

## MADELEINE QUI VEILLAIT
27 janvier 1948

*J'ai dîné chez mon ami le peintre Jean Villeri. Il est plus de onze heures. Le métro me ramène à mon domicile. Je change de rame à la station Trocadéro. Alourdi par une fatigue agréable, j'écoute distraitement résonner mon pas dans le couloir des correspondances. Soudain une jeune femme, qui vient en sens inverse, m'aborde après m'avoir, je crois, longuement dévisagé. Elle m'adresse une demande pour le moins inattendue: "Vous n'auriez pas une feuille de papier à lettres, monsieur?" Sur ma réponse négative et sans doute devant mon air amusé, elle ajoute: "Cela vous paraît drôle?" Je réponds non, certes, ce propos ou un autre...Elle prononce avec une nuance de regret: "Pourtant!" Sa maigreur, sa pâleur et l'éclat de ses yeux sont extrêmes. Elle marche avec cette aisance des mauvais métiers qui est aussi la mienne. Je cherche en vain à cette silhouette fâcheuse quelque beauté. Il est certain que l'ovale du visage, le front, le regard surtout doivent retenir l'attention, troubler. Mais de là à s'enquérir! Je ne songe qu'à fausser compagnie. Je suis arrivé devant la rame de Saint-Cloud et je monte rapidement. Elle s'élance derrière moi. Je fais quelques pas dans le wagon pour m'éloigner et rompre. Sans résultat. À Michel-Ange-Molitor je m'empresse de descendre. Mais le léger pas me poursuit et me rattrape. Le timbre de la voix s'est modifié. Un ton de prière sans humilité. En quelques mots paisibles je précise que les choses doivent en rester là. Elle dit alors: "Vous ne comprenez pas, oh non! Ce n'est pas ce que vous croyez." L'air de la nuit que nous atteignons donne de la grâce à son effronterie: "Me voyez-vous dans les couloirs déserts d'une station, que les gens sont pressés de quitter, proposer la galante aventure?—Où habitez-vous?—Très loin d'ici. Vous ne connaissez pas." Le souvenir de la quête des énigmes, au temps de ma découverte de la vie et de la poésie, me revient à l'esprit. Je le chasse, agacé. "Je ne suis pas tenté par l'impossible comme autrefois (je mens). J'ai trop vu souffrir...(quelle indécence!)" Et sa réponse: "Croire à nouveau ne fait pas qu'il y aura davantage de souffrance. Restez accueillant. Vous ne vous verrez pas mourir." Elle sourit: "Comme la nuit est humide!" Je la sens ainsi. La rue Boileau, d'habitude provinciale et rassurante, est blanche de gelée, mais je cherche en vain la trace des étoiles dans le ciel. J'observe de biais la jeune femme: "Comment vous appelez-vous, mon petit?—Madeleine." À vrai dire, son nom ne m'a pas surpris. J'ai terminé dans l'après-midi* Madeleine à la veilleuse, *inspiré par le tableau de Georges de La Tour dont l'interrogation est si actuelle. Ce poème m'a coûté. Comment ne pas entrevoir, dans cette passante*

## MAGDALENE KEEPING WATCH
*January 27, 1948*

I've just come from a meal at a friend's house, the painter Jean
Villeri. It's close to midnight. I'm riding the métro home. I
change trains at Trocadéro. Slowed by a welcomed fatigue,
I'm vaguely aware of the sound of my footsteps echoing down
the halls. Suddenly, coming head-on, a young woman accosts
me, after, I think, having watched me for quite some time.
Out of the blue, she asks, "Would you happen to have a sheet
of writing paper, sir?" I shake my head no, and doubtless due
to the amused look on my face, she adds, "You think that's
funny?" I stammer no, not in the least, or some such thing.
With a hint of remorse, she says, "But still!" I am struck by
her thinness, her pallor, the brilliance of her eyes. She walks
with the same easy stride of the streetwise, like me. I seek in
her profile some small sign of beauty. No success. For sure her
oval face, her forehead, and, above all, her gaze, should hold
attention, arouse some desire. I'm perplexed. All I can think
of is giving her the slip. Reaching the train for Saint-Cloud,
I quickly board the car. She darts behind. I take a few steps
to move away. No use. At Michel-Ange-Molitor, I rush to get
off. But those light steps pursue me and catch up again. The
tone of her voice has changed. A prayer without submission.
Choosing my words, I softly tell her that things must end
here. She then says, "No, you don't understand. It's not what
you believe." The night air lends grace to her brazenness.
"Here, in deserted halls of a station that people can't wait to
leave, you think I'm proposing a tryst?" "Where do you live?"
"Very far from this place. You wouldn't know." Memories
flood my mind: my quest for enigmas that dates from the
time I discovered life and poetry. Testy, I push aside these
thoughts. "I am no longer tempted to chase after dreams." (I
lie). "I've seen too much pain..." (such conceit). She answers,
"Believing again will not cause more pain. Greet whatever
comes your way. You will not see yourself die." She smiles.
"What a humid night!" I feel it too. Rue Boileau, most days
reassuring and rustic, is white with frost, but I search in vain
for traces of stars. I sneak a look at her face. "Little one, what

opiniâtre, sa vérification? À deux reprises déjà, pour d'autres particulièrement coûteux poèmes, la même aventure m'advint. Je n'ai nulle difficulté à m'en convaincre. L'accès d'une couche profonde d'émotion et de vision est propice au surgissement du grand réel. On ne l'atteint pas sans quelque remerciement de l'oracle. Je ne pense pas qu'il soit absurde de l'affirmer. Je ne suis pas le seul à qui ces rares preuves sont parfois foncièrement accordées. "Madeleine, vous avez été très bonne et très patiente. Allons ensemble, encore, voulez-vous?" Nous marchons dans une intelligence d'ombres parfaite. J'ai pris le bras de la jeune femme et j'éprouve ces similitudes que la sensation de la maigreur éveille. Elles disparaissent presque aussitôt, ne laissant place qu'à l'intense solitude et à la complète faveur à la fois, que je ressentis quand j'eus mis le point final à l'écriture de mon poème. Il est minuit et demi. Avenue de Versailles, la lumière du métro Javel, pâle, monte de terre. "Je vous dis adieu, ici." J'hésite, mais le frêle corps se libère. "Embrassez-moi, que je parte heureuse…" Je prends sa tête dans mes mains et la baise aux yeux et sur les cheveux. Madeleine s'en va, s'efface au bas des marches de l'escalier du métro dont les portes de fer vont être bientôt tirées et sont déjà prêtes.

Je jure que tout ceci est vrai et m'est arrivé, n'étant pas sans amour, comme j'en fais le récit, cette nuit de janvier.

La réalité noble ne se dérobe pas à qui la rencontre pour l'estimer et non pour l'insulter ou la faire prisonnière. Là est l'unique condition que nous ne sommes pas toujours assez purs pour remplir.

is your name?" "Magdalene." In truth, I am not surprised at her name. That very day, I had just completed *Magdalene with Smoking Flame*, inspired by the painting by Georges de La Tour, still on my mind. That poem really took its toll. In this hard-headed passerby, how not to glimpse the approval I sought? Twice, in the past, for equally costly poems, the same events occurred. I convinced myself with ease. Reaching a deep layer of feeling and vision helps the truly real surge forth. To attain this depth, the oracle must be assuaged. I do not think it absurd to affirm this is so. These rare proofs are granted from time to time to others as well as to myself. "Magdalene, you have been very patient and good. Shall we walk together a bit?" We resume our walk in a perfect knowledge of shadows. Taking her arm, I feel the profound sensation evoked by skin and bones. Almost at once it fades, leaving intense loneliness mixed with the sense of complete reward I felt when I penned my poem's final dot. Half past twelve. Avenue de Versailles, and the pale light from Javel Station floats up from the ground. "Here is where I say goodbye." I balk, but her frail body breaks free. "Kiss me so I may leave happy..." I hold her head in my hands and kiss her eyes and hair. Magdalene leaves me, swallowed by stairs of the métro, whose open iron gates will soon close.

I swear all this is true and happened to me, not without love, as I've told the tale, this January night.

Noble reality doesn't retreat from those who meet her to hold her dear—not to offend or confine her. That is the sole condition we're not always pure enough to fulfill.

## ÉROS SUSPENDU

*La nuit avait couvert la moitié de son parcours. L'amas des cieux allait à cette seconde tenir en entier dans mon regard. Je te vis, la première et la seule, divine femelle dans les sphères bouleversées. Je déchirai ta robe d'infini, te ramenai nue sur mon sol. L'humus mobile de la terre fut partout.*

*Nous volons, disent tes servantes, dans l'espace cruel—au chant de ma trompette rouge.*

## EROS SUSPENDED

Night had covered half of its track. The heavens' entire cluster of stars was about to be held in my gaze. I saw you—divine female—the first and only one to arise from tumultuous spheres. I tore off your dress of the infinite, brought you back nude to my soil. Everywhere humus was strewn.

Your servants say we are flying in cruel space—to my red trumpet's tune.

## *LUTTEURS*

*Dans le ciel des hommes, le pain des étoiles me sembla ténébreux et durci, mais dans leurs mains étroites je lus la joute de ces étoiles en invitant d'autres: émigrantes du pont encore rêveuses; j'en recueillis la sueur dorée, et par moi la terre cessa de mourir.*

## COMBATANTS

In the sky of men, the bread of stars seemed to me shadowed
and hard, but I read in their cramped hands the joust of
these stars calling others: dreamy-eyed emigrants still on the
bridge; I collected their golden sweat, and the earth, through
me, ceased to die.

## FRÉQUENCE

Tout le jour, assistant l'homme, le fer a appliqué son torse sur la boue enflammée de la forge. À la longue, leurs jarrets jumeaux ont fait éclater la mince nuit du métal à l'étroit sous la terre.

L'homme sans se hâter quitte le travail. Il plonge une dernière fois ses bras dans le flanc assombri de la rivière. Saura-t-il enfin saisir le bourdon glacé des algues?

# FREQUENCY

All day long, side by side with the man, the iron forced its torso against the flaming mud of the forge. In the end, their twinned muscles unearthed the thin night of metal, bursting free.

The man leaves his work in no rush. He plunges his arms one last time into the stream's darkened flank. Will he know, at last, how to grasp the algae's icy hum?

## RECOURS AU RUISSEAU

*Sur l'aire du courant, dans les joncs agités, j'ai retracé ta ville. Les maçons au large feutre sont venus; ils se sont appliqués à suivre mon mouvement. Ils ne concevaient pas ma construction. Leur compétence s'alarmait.*

*Je leur ai dit que, confidante, tu attendais proche de là que j'eusse atteint la demie de ma journée pour connaître mon travail. À ce moment, notre satisfaction commune l'effacerait, nous le recommencerions plus haut, identiquement, dans la certitude de notre amour. Railleurs, ils se sont écartés. Je voyais, tandis qu'ils remettaient leur veste de toile, le gravier qui brillait dans le ciel du ruisseau et dont je n'avais, moi, nul besoin.*

## RECOURSE TO OUR STREAM

On the water's surface, amid the swaying rushes, I re-traced your town. The masons arrived in their wide-brimmed felt hats; they strove to follow my strokes. They could not conceive my construction. Their faith in their skills fell apart.

You were waiting nearby, assured, to see what I would design in half a day's work. I told them so. Only then would we splash it away in our common delight, would begin to build again, unchanged, on higher ground, in our certain love. Mocking, they moved aside. As they reached for their sailcloth jackets, I saw no need for the gravel that blazed in the sky of the stream.

## ANOUKIS ET PLUS TARD JEANNE

*Je te découvrirai à ceux que j'aime, comme un long éclair de chaleur, aussi inexplicablement que tu t'es montrée à moi, Jeanne, quand, un matin s'astreignant à ton dessein, tu nous menas de roc en roc jusqu'à cette fin de soi qu'on appelle un sommet. Le visage à demi masqué par ton bras replié, les doigts de ta main sollicitant ton épaule, tu nous offris, au terme de notre ascension, une ville, les souffrances et la qualification d'un génie, la surface égarée d'un désert, et le tournant circonspect d'un fleuve sur la rive duquel des bâtisseurs s'interrogeaient. Mais je te suis vite revenu, Faucille, car tu consumais ton offrande. Et ni le temps, ni la beauté, ni le hasard qui débride le coeur ne pouvaient se mesurer avec toi.*

*J'ai ressuscité alors mon antique richesse, notre richesse à tous, et dominant ce que demain détruira, je me suis souvenu que tu étais Anoukis l'Étreigneuse, aussi fantastiquement que tu étais Jeanne, la soeur de mon meilleur ami, et aussi inexplicablement que tu étais l'Étrangère dans l'esprit de ce misérable carillonneur dont le père répétait autrefois que Van Gogh était fou.*

Saint-Rémy-des-Alpilles, 18 septembre 1949

## ANOUKIS AND LATER JEANNE

Like a long stroke of lightning igniting the sky, I'll unveil you to those I love, Jeanne, as inexplicably as you showed yourself to me on a morning of your design—when you led us from rock to rock, up to that summit, the end of self. With your face half-masked by your raised bent arm, your hand's fingers shoulder-bound, you offered a town for our ascent, the trials and terms of a genius, a desert's strayed sands, and the circumspect bend of a river where builders, questioning, stood on its bank. I turned right back to you, my Sickle, before you consumed all of your offering. Nothing could ever compare to you—neither time, nor beauty, nor luck that unbridles the heart.

I revived then my ancient treasures, our common riches of gods, and subduing what the coming days will destroy, I recalled you were Anoukis the Embracer, as amazingly as you were Jeanne, sister of my best friend, and as inexplicably as you were the Stranger who frazzled that pitiful ringer of bells whose father would rave that Van Gogh was crazed.

*Saint-Rémy-des-Alpilles, September 18, 1949*

*Anoukis (Anuket) was the Egyptian goddess whose role was to channel the Nile. Her name means "to embrace." Van Gogh stayed at the asylum in Saint-Rémy for a year, where he completed numerous paintings.*

*YVONNE*
La Soif hospitalière

*Qui l'entendit jamais se plaindre?*

*Nulle autre qu'elle n'aurait pu boire sans mourir les quarante fatigues,*
*Attendre, loin devant, ceux qui viendront après;*
*De l'éveil au couchant sa manoeuvre était mâle.*

*Qui a creusé le puits et hisse l'eau gisante*
*Risque son coeur dans l'écart de ses mains.*

## YVONNE

*Welcoming thirst*

Who heard her ever complain?

Only she could drink and survive forty rounds,
Could wait, worlds beyond, for those coming next;
From waking to sunset, used tactics of men.

Whoever dug the shaft and raises water from rest
Risks her heart in the well of her hands.

*This poem was written in memory of Yvonne Zervos, one of Char's
intimate friends. She befriended many poets and painters of her time.*

## LA SORGUE
### Chanson pour Yvonne

Rivière trop tôt partie, d'une traite, sans compagnon,
Donne aux enfants de mon pays le visage de ta passion.

Rivière où l'éclair finit et où commence ma maison,
Qui roule aux marches d'oubli la rocaille de ma raison.

Rivière, en toi terre est frisson, soleil anxiété.
Que chaque pauvre dans sa nuit fasse son pain de ta moisson.

Rivière souvent punie, rivière à l'abandon.

Rivière des apprentis à la calleuse condition,
Il n'est vent qui ne fléchisse à la crête de tes sillons.

Rivière de l'âme vide, de la guenille et du soupçon,
Du vieux malheur qui se dévide, de l'ormeau, de la compassion.

Rivière des farfelus, des fiévreux, des équarrisseurs,
Du soleil lâchant sa charrue pour s'acoquiner au menteur.

Rivière des meilleurs que soi, rivière des brouillards éclos,
De la lampe qui désaltère l'angoisse autour de son chapeau.

Rivière des égards au songe, rivière qui rouille le fer,
Où les étoiles ont cette ombre qu'elles refusent à la mer.

Rivière des pouvoirs transmis et du cri embouquant les eaux,
De l'ouragan qui mord la vigne et annonce le vin nouveau.

Rivière au coeur jamais détruit dans ce monde fou de prison,
Garde-nous violent et ami des abeilles de l'horizon.

# THE SORGUE

*Song for Yvonne*

River gone too soon, in a surge, without friend,
Give your passion's face to the youth of my native land.

River where lightning ends and my home begins,
That rolls my reason's loose stones to oblivion's brink.

River, earth shudders, sun frets in your depths.
Let each poor man in his night make, of your harvest, his bread.

River often chastised, river disowned.

River of rags and suspicion, of hollowed souls,
Of elm trees, compassion, of old despair that unfolds.

River of those apprenticed to calloused states,
No wind stands up to the crests of your wake.

River of knackers, the fevered, and fools,
The sun dropping its plow to sink to the level of lies.

River of those who best us, river of fogs newly hatched,
Of the lamp quenching dread around its hat.

River that rusts iron, river revering dreams,
Where stars hold that umber they refuse to the sea.

River of transferred powers, of mouthed watery cries,
Of hurricanes tearing through vineyards, proclaiming new wines.

River with heart never wrecked in these prison-crazed days,
Keep us raging and friends to the stormed horizon's bees.

*The Sorgue River springs up in Vaucluse, France—birthplace of René Char.*

## DÉCLARER SON NOM

*J'avais dix ans. La Sorgue m'enchâssait. Le soleil chantait les heures sur le sage cadran des eaux. L'insouciance et la douleur avaient scellé le coq de fer sur le toit des maisons et se supportaient ensemble. Mais quelle roue dans le coeur de l'enfant aux aguets tournait plus fort, tournait plus vite que celle du moulin dans son incendie blanc?*

## PROCLAIMING ONE'S NAME

I was ten. I was set in the waves of the Sorgue like a gem. The sun crowed the hours on the water's wise dial. Grief and insouciance, bracing each other, had sealed the rooster-shaped vane on the roofs of homes. But what wheel in the wary child's heart turned harder and faster than that of the mill, churning its white fire?

## L'ADOLESCENT SOUFFLETÉ

*Les mêmes coups qui l'envoyaient au sol le lançaient en même temps loin devant sa vie, vers les futures années où, quand il saignerait, ce ne serait plus à cause de l'iniquité d'un seul. Tel l'arbuste que réconfortent ses racines et qui presse ses rameaux meurtris contre son fût résistant, il descendait ensuite à reculons dans le mutisme de ce savoir et dans son innocence. Enfin il s'échappait, s'enfuyait et devenait souverainement heureux. Il atteignait la prairie et la barrière des roseaux dont il cajolait la vase et percevait le sec frémissement. Il semblait que ce que la terre avait produit de plus noble et de plus persévérant, l'avait, en compensation, adopté.*

*Il recommencerait ainsi jusqu'au moment où, la nécessité de rompre disparue, il se tiendrait droit et attentif parmi les hommes, à la fois plus vulnérable et plus fort.*

## THE SLAPPED ADOLESCENT

He was hurled to the ground by the same unjust blows that
hurtled him far ahead in his life, toward future years when
one person alone could no longer make him bleed. Like the
small shrub that draws succor from roots, clasping bruised
branches against its resolute core, he backed away mute into
what he knew and into his innocence. Finally freed and filled
with sovereign joy, he fled to the meadow and reached the
wall of reeds whose dry trembling he watched and whose mud
he cajoled. What was noblest and most enduring on earth
seemed to adopt him, as if to make amends.

And so it would start again. He knew one day he would hold
his ground, attentive and standing tall among men—more at
risk, more resistant.

## JEU MUET

Avec mes dents
J'ai pris la vie
Sur le couteau de ma jeunesse.
Avec mes lèvres aujourd'hui,
Avec mes lèvres seulement...

Courte parvenue,
La fleur des talus,
Le dard d'Orion,
Est réapparu.

## MUTE GAME

With my teeth
I have seized life
Upon the knife of my youth.
With my lips today,
With my lips alone...

Briefly come,
Bloom of the slopes,
Orion's spear
Has reappeared.

## VOICI

Voici l'écumeur de mémoire
Le vapeur des flaques mineures
Entouré de linges fumants
Étoile rose et rose blanche

Ô caresses savantes, ô lèvres inutiles!

# HERE

Here, skimmer of memory's cream
Steamship of mined pools
Enclosed by linen's steamy reek
Rose star, white rose

O knowing caresses, o useless lips!

## TU OUVRES LES YEUX

*Tu ouvres les yeux sur la carrière d'ocre inexploitable*
*Tu bois dans un épieu l'eau souterraine*
*Tu es pour la feuille hypnotisée dans l'espace*
*À l'approche de l'invisible serpent*
*Ô ma diaphane digitale!*

## YOU OPEN YOUR EYES

You open your eyes to an ocher quarry that cannot be mined
You drink in speared underground streams
You are under the spell of the hanging leaf
Stirred by the snake's muted approach
O my translucent foxglove!

*FONTIS*

*Le raisin a pour patrie*
*Les doigts de la vendangeuse.*
*Mais elle, qui a-t-elle,*
*Passé l'étroit sentier de la vigne cruelle?*

*Le rosaire de la grappe;*
*Au soir le très haut fruit couchant qui saigne*
*La dernière étincelle.*

## FONTIS

For native land, grapes can claim
The hands of the girl who culls
What grows, but who is waiting for her
Past the heartless vine's narrow path?

Rosary made by each cluster;
Topmost fruit, setting, bleeds
One final spark at dusk.

*Wine bearing the Château Fontis label comes from one of the highest points in Médoc, France.*

## LES NUITS JUSTES

Avec un vent plus fort,
Une lampe moins obscure,
Nous devons trouver la halte
Où la nuit dira "Passez";
Et nous saurons que c'est vrai
Quand le verre s'éteindra.

Ô terre devenue tendre!
Ô branche où mûrit ma joie!
La gueule du ciel est blanche.
Ce qui miroite, là, c'est toi,
Ma chute, mon amour, mon saccage.

# RIGHTEOUS NIGHTS

With a harder wind,
A lamp less dim,
We must find the checkpoint
Where night will say "Pass";
And we will know this is right
When the glass goes dark.

O soil now so soft!
Branch of my ripening joy!
The sky's maw is white.
You are what gleams—
My falling, my love, my defeat.

*LE CARREAU*

*Pures pluies, femmes attendues,*
*La face que vous essuyez,*
*De verre voué aux tourments,*
*Est la face du révolté;*
*L'autre, la vitre de l'heureux,*
*Frissonne devant le feu de bois.*

*Je vous aime mystères jumeaux,*
*Je touche à chacun de vous;*
*J'ai mal et je suis léger.*

# THE WINDOWPANE

Pure downpours, long-awaited women,
The surface rubbed dry—
Glaze twisted in anguish—
Reveals the rebel's face;
Turned inward, content, the other glass
Shivers before the brushwood fire.

I love you both, mysterious twins,
I touch each of you;
I ache; I am weightless.

## PYRÉNÉES

Montagne des grands abusés,
Au sommet de vos tours fiévreuses
Faiblit la dernière clarté.

Rien que le vide et l'avalanche,
La détresse et le regret!

Tous ces troubadours mal-aimés
Ont vu blanchir dans un été
Leur doux royaume pessimiste.

Ah! la neige est inexorable
Qui aime qu'on souffre à ses pieds,
Qui veut que l'on meure glacé
Quand on a vécu dans les sables.

## PYRENEES

Mountain chain of misled greats,
Atop your fevered peaks
The last light fails.

Only anguish and avalanche,
Rift and regret.

These minstrels full of ache
Have seen their meek kingdom fade—
Hopeless and blanched in one summer.

Ah! The snow never forgives—
Loves us to writhe in pain,
Wants us to die, bodies glazed,
When we have survived desert sands.

## VIVANTE DEMAIN

Par la grande échappée du mur
Je t'ai reçue votive des mains de l'hiver

Je te regardais traversant les anneaux de sable des cuirasses
Comme la génération des mélancoliques le préau des jeux

Sur l'herbe de plomb
Sur l'herbe de mâchefer
Sur l'herbe jamais essoufflée
Hors de laquelle la ressemblance des brûlures avec leur fatalité n'est jamais parfaite
Faisons l'amour.

## ALIVE TOMORROW

Through the gap in the wall
I took you in—votive—from winter's hands

I watched you crossing the armored waves of sand—
Generation of brooders crossing the playground

On leaden grass
On grass of slag
On grass never gasping for breath
Past where degrees of burn and their fate are never exactly paired
Let us make love.

## POUR QU'UNE FORÊT...

*Pour qu'une forêt soit superbe*
*Il lui faut l'âge et l'infini.*
*Ne mourez pas trop vite, amis*
*Du casse-croûte sous la grêle.*
*Sapins qui couchez dans nos lits,*
*Éternisez nos pas sur l'herbe.*

Alsace, 1939

## NO FOREST...

No forest can ever be great
Without age and the infinite.
Do not die too quickly, friends
Of picnics under the hail.
Pines, you who box our sleep,
Immortalize our footprints in the grass.

*Alsace, 1939*

## CHAÎNE

*Le grand bûcher des alliances*
*Sous le spiral ciel d'échec*
*C'est l'hiver en barque pourrie*
*Des compagnons solides aux compagnes liquides*
*Des lits de mort sous les écorces*
*Dans les profondeurs vacantes de la terre*
*Les arcs forgent un nouveau nombre d'ailes*
*Les labours rayonnants adorent les guérisseurs détrempés*
*Sur la paille des fatalistes*
*L'écume d'astre coule tout allumée*
*Il n'y a pas d'absence irremplaçable.*

# CHAIN

The great wood pyre of leagues
Under the spiral sky of defeat
It is winter's rotted skiff
From solid comrades to liquid lovers
Deathbeds beneath the trees
In the vacant depths of the earth
Arches forge a fresh supply of wings
Tilled fields radiate, worship sweat-drenched healers
On the straw of those who believe in fate
Flows the foam of ignited stars
There is no absence that cannot be replaced.

## L'INSTITUTEUR RÉVOQUÉ

*Trois personnages d'une banalité éprouvée s'abordent à des titres poétiques divers* (du feu, je vous prie, quelle heure avez-vous, à combien de lieues la prochaine ville?), *dans un paysage indifférent et engagent une conversation dont les échos ne nous parviendront jamais. Devant vous, le champ de dix hectares dont je suis le laboureur, le sang secret et la pierre catastrophique. Je ne vous laisse rien à penser.*

## THE DISMISSED INSTRUCTOR

Three fictional speakers of proven banality greet each other with varied poetic devices *(please, got a light, how many leagues to the closest town, what's the time?)*. In an average locale they engage in chitchat whose echoes will never come close to our ears. Before you, the metered field of ten hectares. I am its plowman, its secret blood, its calamitous stone. I leave you nothing to fill your mind.

## TOUTE VIE

*Toute vie qui doit poindre*
*achève un blessé.*
*Voici l'arme,*
*rien,*
*vous, moi, réversiblement*
*ce livre,*
*et l'énigme*
*qu'à votre tour vous deviendrez*
*dans le caprice amer des sables.*

# EVERY LIFE

As each new life bursts through,
one of the wounded dies.
Here is the weapon:
nothing,
me, interchangeably you,
this text,
and the riddle
that you, in turn, will become
in the bitter caprice of the sands.

## VERS L'ARBRE-FRÈRE AUX JOURS COMPTÉS

*Harpe brève des mélèzes,*
*Sur l'éperon de mousse et de dalles en germe*
*—Façade des forêts où casse le nuage—,*
*Contrepoint du vide auquel je crois.*

# TO BROTHER-TREE OF NUMBERED DAYS

Larch tree's brief harp
On the spur of moss and flagstones in seed
—Forest's façade where clouds break apart—
Counterpoint paired to the void in which I believe.

## *ÉPRISE*

*Chaque carreau de la fenêtre est un morceau de mur en face, chaque pierre scellée du mur une recluse bienheureuse qui nous éclaire matin, soir, de poudre d'or à ses sables mélangée. Notre logis va son histoire. Le vent aime à y tailler.*

*L'étroit espace où se volatilise cette fortune est une petite rue au-dessous dont nous n'apercevons pas le pavé. Qui y passe emporte ce qu'il désire.*

## IN LOVE

Each square of the window's pane is a piece of the facing wall; each stone sealed in the wall—blissful recluse—colors our dawns and evenings with gold dust mixed with sands. Our dwelling lives out its tale, through which winds love to slice.

Below, a narrow street where this fortune evaporates—pavement beyond our sight. Let anyone passing reclaim what he desires.

## LA PASSE DE LYON

*Je viendrai par le pont le plus distant de Bellecour, afin de vous laisser le loisir d'arriver la première. Vous me conduirez à la fenêtre où vos yeux voyagent, d'où vos faveurs plongent quand votre liberté échange sa lumière avec celle des météores, la vôtre demeurant et la leur se perdant. Avec mes songes, avec ma guerre, avec mon baiser, sous le mûrier ressuscité, dans le répit des filatures, je m'efforcerai d'isoler votre conquête d'un savoir antérieur, autre que le mien. Que l'avenir vous entraîne avec des convoiteurs différents, j'y céderai, mais pour le seul chef-d'oeuvre!*

*Flamme à l'excès de son destin, qui tantôt m'amoindrit et tantôt me complète, vous émergez à l'instant près de moi, dauphine, salamandre, et je ne vous suis rien.*

## REACHING LYON

To let you arrive first, at your leisure, I'll come by way of the furthest bridge from Bellecour. Your eyes, looking out toward the distant roofs, will guide me right to your window, the one from where your favors plunge when your brazenness trades its light with meteors—yours everlasting and theirs forever lost. With my daydreams, my war, with my kiss, under cover of mulberry trees newly revived, in the lull of spinning mills, I'll strive to strip from your conquest a prior knowledge, other than my own. That the future may lead you to other pursuers, I shall consent, but only for art's sake!

A passion transcending its fate—now shrinks me, now makes me whole—you rise near to me, queen-to-be, mythical lizard, fabled to live in fire—and I am nothing to you.

## LA COMPAGNE DU VANNIER

*Je t'aimais. J'aimais ton visage de source raviné par l'orage et le chiffre de ton domaine enserrant mon baiser. Certains se confient à une imagination toute ronde. Aller me suffit. J'ai rapporté du désespoir un panier si petit, mon amour, qu'on a pu le tresser en osier.*

# THE BASKET WEAVER'S WIFE

I loved you. I loved your face—spring fluted by high winds and rain—and the cipher made by your mouth sealing my kiss. Some put their faith in perfectly round illusions. For me, just going will do. From despair I brought back so small a basket, my love, they wove it from willow.

## *LA FAUVETTE DES ROSEAUX*

*L'arbre le plus exposé à l'oeil du fusil n'est pas un arbre pour son aile. La remuante est prévenue: elle se fera muette en le traversant. La perche de saule happée est à l'instant cédée par l'ongle de la fugitive. Mais dans la touffe de roseaux où elle amerrit, quelles cavatines! C'est ici qu'elle chante. Le monde entier le sait.*

*Été, rivière, espaces, amants dissimulés, toute une lune d'eau, la fauvette répète: "Libre, libre, libre, libre..."*

## SONGBIRD AMONG THE REEDS

Not for her wings, the tree most exposed to the gunner's eye. Forewarned, she will cross in wary silence, willow's perch reached and released by her fugitive claw. But landed now in the stream's tuft of reeds, what runs and roulades! Here she sings and the whole world knows.

Summer, river, open spaces, secret loves—a full watery moon—the songbird trills: "Free, free, free, free..."

## L'AMOUREUSE EN SECRET

Elle a mis le couvert et mené à la perfection ce à quoi son amour assis en face d'elle parlera bas tout à l'heure, en la dévisageant. Cette nourriture semblable à l'anche d'un hautbois.

Sous la table, ses chevilles nues caressent à présent la chaleur du bien-aimé, tandis que des voix qu'elle n'entend pas la complimentent. Le rayon de la lampe emmêle, tisse sa distraction sensuelle.

Un lit, très loin, sait-elle, patiente et tremble dans l'exil des draps odorants, comme un lac de montagne qui ne sera jamais abandonné.

## SECRET LOVE

She has set the table, refined what her love, seated across, will speak softly of, looking deep into her eyes. Food like an oboe's reed.

Under the table's cover now, her bare ankles stroke her lover's warmth, while voices she does not hear sing her praises. The lamp's stream of light tangles, weaves voluptuous daydreams.

She knows a bed—far, far away—waits patiently, trembling in exile of sheets fragrant with musk, like a  mountain lake that will never be forsaken.

## LES LICHENS

*Je marchais parmi les bosses d'une terre écurée, les haleines secrètes, les plantes sans mémoire. La montagne se levait, flacon empli d'ombre qu'étreignait par instant le geste de la soif. Ma trace, mon existence se perdaient. Ton visage glissait à reculons devant moi. Ce n'était qu'une tache à la recherche de l'abeille qui la ferait fleur et la dirait vivante. Nous allions nous séparer. Tu demeurerais sur le plateau des arômes et je pénétrerais dans le jardin du vide. Là, sous la sauvegarde des rochers, dans la plénitude du vent, je demanderais à la nuit véritable de disposer de mon sommeil pour accroître ton bonheur. Et tous les fruits t'appartiendraient.*

## LICHENS

I was roaming the knolls of a scoured land, through secret breaths and plants with no past. The mountain rose up—shadow-filled flask briefly embraced by the gesture of thirst. My existence, all traces of me, were slipping away. Your face, looking back, was gliding ahead, a speck in search of the bee to inspire a bloom and charm it alive. We were going to separate. You would remain on the perfumed ridge and I would sink below, into the garden of rift. There, under cover of rocks and in lavish wind, I would gift my sleep to the one true night to deepen your bliss. And all fruits would be yours to claim.

## DEVANCIER

*J'ai reconnu dans un rocher la mort fuguée et mensurable, le lit ouvert de ses petits comparses sous la retraite d'un figuier. Nul signe de tailleur: chaque matin de la terre ouvrait ses ailes au bas des marches de la nuit.*

*Sans redite, allégé de la peur des hommes, je creuse dans l'air ma tombe et mon retour.*

## ANCESTOR

I have recognized death—fugal and measured—inside a rock, and the open bed of its little assistants beneath the shade of a fig tree. No sign of the one who cuts stone; each of earth's mornings would open its wings at the foot of night's steps.

Without refrain, freed of mortal dread, I dig in the air my grave and my return.

## COURBET: LES CASSEURS DE CAILLOUX

*Sable paille ont la vie douce le vin ne s'y brise pas*
*Du colombier ils récoltent les plumes*
*De la goulotte ils ont la langue avide*
*Ils retardent l'orteil des filles*
*Dont ils percent les chrysalides*
*Le sang bien souffert tombe dans l'anecdote de leur légèreté*

*Nous dévorons la peste du feu gris dans la rocaille*
*Quand on intrigue à la commune*
*C'est encore sur les chemins ruinés qu'on est le mieux*
*Là les tomates des vergers l'air nous les porte au crépuscule*
*Avec l'oubli de la méchanceté prochaine de nos femmes*
*Et l'aigreur de la soif tassée aux genoux*

*Fils cette nuit nos travaux de poussière*
*Seront visibles dans le ciel*
*Déjà l'huile du plomb ressuscite.*

## COURBET: THE STONE BREAKERS

Sand and straw live gently, soften the fall of wine
They gather quills from dovecotes
Theirs is the gullet's greedy tongue
They slow bare toes of girls
Chrysalids pierced
Lighthearted they catch the well-suffered blood

In the stones we devour the grey fire's plague
While in town they conspire and scheme
Still nothing beats these ruined roads
Where twilight air bears the scent of tomato vines
Forgiveness for outbursts soon to come from our wives
And the bite of thirst shoved down to our knees
Son, our labors of dust
Will be seen tonight in the sky
Already the oil is rising to life from lead.

*This poem refers to a painting completed in 1849 by Gustave Courbet, which depicts an older man and a younger one working side by side on a road.*

# ACKNOWLEDGMENTS

*AGNI:* "Ancestor," "Lichens"

*ARTS & LETTERS:* "Anoukis and Later Jeanne,"
"Eros Suspended," "Proclaiming One's Name," "Reaching Lyon"

*ASHEVILLE POETRY REVIEW:* "Courbet: The Stone Breakers,"
"Frequency," "The Oriole"

*CIRCUMFERENCE:* "The Dismissed Instructor"

*COLORADO REVIEW:* "Évadné," "The Windowpane"

*CRAZYHORSE:* "Chain," "Combatants," "In Love,"
"Why the Day Steals By"

*DENVER QUARTERLY:* "Magdalene with Smoking Flame,"
"Marthe," "Secret Love," "Wind on Furlough"

*GUERNICA MAGAZINE:* "Mute Game," "The Slapped
Adolescent"

*INTERIM:* "Enduring Invisible," "Magdalene Keeping Watch,"
"Mumbling," "Pyrenees," "Recourse to Our Stream," "Threshold"

*INNISFREE:* "Allegiance," "Fontis," "The Sorgue,"

*THE MARLBORO REVIEW:* "Inebriation," "The Swift"

*POETRY INTERNATIONAL:* "Courbet: The Stone Breakers,"
"Four Who Charm," "Lightning Victory," "To Brother-Tree of
Numbered Days"

*PUERTO DEL SOL:* "Not Eternal Nor Temporal"

*SOUTHERN HUMANITIES REVIEW:* "Lied of the Fig Tree"

*SYCAMORE REVIEW:* "Here," "Yvonne"

*WEST BRANCH:* "The Basket Weaver's Wife," "Every Life,"
"No Forest," "Songbird Among the Reeds"

*WITNESS:* "Alive Tomorrow," "Invitation"

*With unending gratitude to Jeffrey Levine for helping conceive this book in Vancouver
and bringing it into the world. Many thanks to those who nurtured these translations
along the way: Carol Quinn, Tina Daub, Kim Roberts, Liz Poliner, Renée Raffini,
Christine Vest, and Iran Amin, and especially to Jim Schley for his expert editing.
Special thanks and love to Rachel Carlson, for her precise proofreading, as well as to
Ted Miller, for taking care of my every "Char need."*

## OTHER BOOKS FROM TUPELO PRESS:

*This Nest, Swift Passerine,* Dan Beachy-Quick

*Cloisters,* Kristin Bock

*Modern History,* Christopher Buckley

*staring at the animal,* John Cross

*Psalm,* Carol Ann Davis

*Orpheus on the Red Line,* Theodore Deppe

*Spill,* Michael Chitwood

*Then, Something,* Patricia Fargnoli

*Calendars,* Annie Finch

*Do the Math: Forms,* Emily Galvin

*Other Fugitives & Other Strangers,* Rigoberto González

*Keep This Forever,* Mark Halliday

*Inflorescence,* Sarah Hannah

*The Us,* Joan Houlihan

*Red Summer,* Amaud Jamaul Johnson

*Dancing in Odessa,* Ilya Kaminsky

*Ardor,* Karen An-hwei Lee

*Dismal Rock,* Davis McCombs

*Biogeography,* Sandra Meek

*Flinch of Song,* Jennifer Militello

*At the Drive-In Volcano,* Aimee Nezhukumatathil

*The Beginning of the Fields,* Angela Shaw

*Selected Poems, 1970–2005,* Floyd Skloot

*Nude in Winter,* Francine Sterle

*Embryos & Idiots,* Larissa Szporluk

*Archicembalo,* G.C. Waldrep

*This Sharpening,* Ellen Doré Watson

*The Book of Whispering in the Projection Booth,*
  Joshua Marie Wilkinson

*Narcissus,* Cecilia Woloch

*American Linden,* Matthew Zapruder

*Monkey Lightning,* Martha Zweig

See our complete backlist at www.tupelopress.org.